David the Shepherd King

Text by Jenny Robertson
Illustrations by Alan Parry

Scripture Union/Ladybird

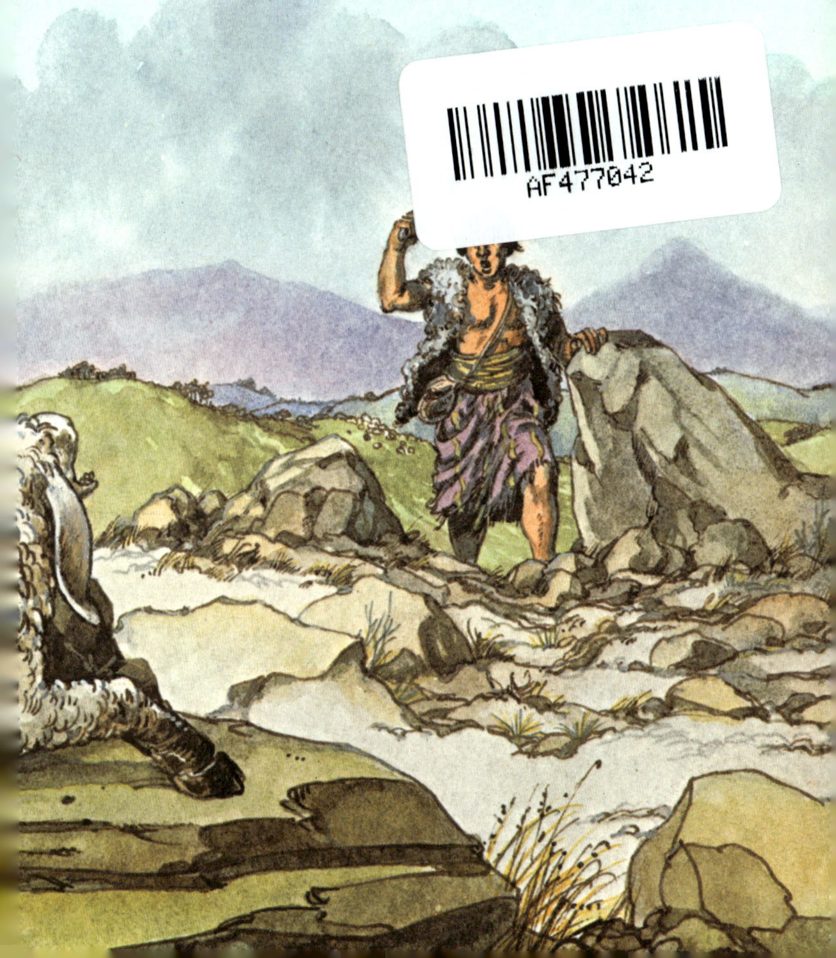

After Saul the king of Israel disobeyed God he fell into such black and angry moods that he couldn't rule the country properly.

At last God said that he would have to take the kingdom away from Saul, and he told his servant Samuel to choose a new king. This was dangerous because if Saul heard about it, he would kill Samuel, so the old man had to be very careful.

'Go to Bethlehem,' God told him. 'A man called Jesse lives there and I have chosen one of his sons to be king. Take a calf and sacrifice it to me there so that Saul won't be suspicious, and I will tell you what else to do.'

So Samuel went to Bethlehem and invited Jesse and his sons to the sacrifice. Jesse's eldest son was strong and handsome – Samuel would have chosen him for king at once, but God said 'no'. It was the same with his six younger brothers – God didn't want any of them to be king.

'Haven't you any more children?' Samuel asked.

'There's my youngest, David, but he's looking after the sheep,' replied Jesse. He sent a servant to fetch David.

'I like the look of him,' Samuel thought, watching David's eager, flushed face. 'Could this be the one?'

'Yes,' came God's answer. 'Pour oil on his head now as a sign that I have chosen him to be king.'

Samuel poured oil on David's bent head. David looked up. His eyes shone.

'This young man loves God,' Samuel thought. 'God will help him to be the right sort of king.'

No one but Samuel knew that David was the new king.

Soon after this Israel's enemies, the Philistines, attacked Saul and his army. David's brothers had to go to fight, but David stayed at home to look after the sheep. From time to time Jesse would send him to Saul's camp to find out how his brothers were and take them some extra food.

One day when David arrived he found the whole army lined up watching one of the Philistines, a massive giant in heavy bronze armour. He was strutting up and down the valley between the two armies, jeering at Saul's men.

'Choose a man to fight me. We'll decide the battle with a single blow,' he yelled. But none of the Israelites dared fight the Philistine whose name was Goliath.

'Who does that man think he is?' demanded David. 'He's not only insulting our army, he's insulting God, too.'

'What do you know about it?' growled David's eldest brother. 'Get back to your sheep, you cheeky brat!'

'Can't I even ask a simple question?' returned David. 'Is the king offering a reward to the man who kills that giant?' he went on.

'Yes, he is,' put in one of the soldiers. 'Are you interested?'

Everyone laughed. Someone overheard what was going on and told Saul. The king sent for David.

King Saul knew David because once before, when Saul was very unhappy, David had come to his fortress and played his harp and sung to the king.

'Why, it's the shepherd!' the king exclaimed. 'What do you want, David?'

'Your Majesty, I'm not scared of that Philistine. I'll go and fight him.'

'You, David? No, you can't possibly do that,' replied Saul. 'You're too young. He's far bigger than you, and besides he's a trained soldier.'

'Your Majesty, I take my father's sheep high in the hills. Often mountain lions or bears come and try to snatch lambs from the flock. I fight them with my own bare hands. I've grabbed lambs right out of the lions' jaws. I've killed lions and bears, sir, and I'll kill this

Philistine, too. God helped me then and he'll keep me safe now!'

'All right, David,' Saul said. 'Go and fight the giant, and may God help you! You'd better take my armour.'

The king put his helmet on David's head and gave him his armour and sword, but David didn't want to use them.

'I'm sorry, sir,' he said, 'But I've never fought with these weapons before. I don't feel happy with them.' So he took off all the armour. Then he picked up his shepherd's stick and his sling and, choosing five smooth stones from the stream that ran through the camp, he walked down into the valley to meet Goliath.

The Philistine laughed. 'Hey, they've sent a young lad to fight me! What do you think I am? A dog to be chased off with your stick?' He began to curse David in the name of his god, but David yelled back, 'You've got a spear, a sword and a javelin to fight me with,

but I'm going to fight you with the help of
God, and he's stronger than you or your
army.'

Furious, Goliath strode towards David, who
quickly slipped a stone into his sling and
hurled it at the Philistine. It hit his forehead
and the giant reeled back and fell heavily.
David jumped on his body, tugged Goliath's
heavy iron sword out of its sheath and cut off
his head. Then the Philistines fled in confusion
and the cheering Israelites chased them all the
way back to their own country. It was a
complete victory!

Saul made David one of his captains that very day and no one was more delighted than Saul's son, Prince Jonathan, who was a brave soldier.

'I'll never forget today as long as I live!' said Jonathan. 'Now your father will have to look for another shepherd, though it won't be easy to find anyone as brave as you! Let's be friends, shall we, David?' Jonathan took off his royal robe and put it on David. Then he gave the shepherd his own armour and weapons: his sword and bow and arrows and belt.

'Take them, David, they're yours now,' declared Jonathan. He promised to be friends with David for ever.

    After the battle the women came out of their villages to meet Saul, dancing round him, shaking their tambourines and singing to celebrate the victory, but the words they sang made Saul jealous.

    'Saul has killed thousands of men, but David has killed tens of thousands!'

    'They'll make David king instead of me!' muttered Saul. He rode home in a very bad temper and from then on he was too jealous of David ever to trust him again.

The next day Saul was in one of his black moods and David sat beside him, playing his harp. Suddenly Saul grabbed a spear and hurled it at David. He dodged in time and the spear stuck in the wall, but Saul still wanted to

kill David. He sent him to fight against the Philistines, hoping he would be killed but David led the army so well that he won every battle and became more popular than ever.

Saul was now so jealous that he tried to get Jonathan's help to kill David. Jonathan was always loyal to his father but he spoke up bravely for David. Saul listened to him and promised not to hurt David any more, but before long he was plotting against him again. David knew his life was in danger, although Jonathan couldn't believe that his father had broken his promise.

Together they made up a plan to find out if Saul really was plotting against David, for David knew that Jonathan was the only person he could trust.

'You hide behind the rock,' Jonathan told David. 'I'll find out how my father feels about you and I'll come back here. I'll bring my arrows and pretend I'm shooting at a target for practice. If you hear me tell my servant that the arrows have fallen beyond the target you'll know that my father really is planning to kill you.'

When Jonathan tried to talk to the king about David, Saul turned on him furiously.

'That shepherd's trying to steal my throne and he's taken you in completely, you fool. Don't you realise that you'll never be king as long as David's alive?' In his rage Saul tried to kill Jonathan, too, but he slipped away with a servant boy and went to find David. Out in the field he started shooting his arrows near the rock.

'Look, the arrow's fallen further on. Run and find it,' Jonathan called to his servant.

As soon as the boy was out of sight David ran to Jonathan. He knelt down and bowed to the ground three times before the prince. They were both in tears as they said good-bye to each other.

'We'll always be friends and so will our children,' Jonathan promised. 'God go with you, David.'

Then David went into hiding and Jonathan returned slowly home.

Saul was furious when he heard that Jonathan had helped David to escape. He set out with his army and chased David. Before he could find him a small band of outlaws and men who did not want to serve Saul joined David. They lived in secret caves in the hills. One day a man appeared in the opening of the very cave where David was hiding.

'It's the king,' whispered David's men. 'Come on, David. This is your chance. Kill him now.'

David crept forward, sword in hand, the very sword he had used to cut off Goliath's head. He stopped behind Saul, bent forward and slashed a corner off the king's long cloak while his men stared dumbfounded.

'I'll never harm Saul,' David explained when he rejoined his men. 'God chose him to rule us.'

So Saul walked out of the cave safely, with no idea of what danger he had been in!

David slipped outside after him holding the frayed cloth in his hand.

'Your Majesty!' he called.

At the sound of his voice Saul spun round in amazement. David dropped to his knees. 'Sir, why do you keep on trying to kill me! I could have killed you just now, but I only cut a corner off your cloak. Look, here it is! Doesn't that convince you? You are my king, sir, and I'll never harm a hair of your head.'

'Oh, David, can that really be you?' Saul exclaimed. Suddenly he burst into tears.

'I realise how wrong I've been about you. I won't try to hurt you any more.'

But Saul soon forgot his promise, and sent his army out after David.

Meanwhile the Philistines had marched against Israel. This time they defeated Saul's army easily. Saul and Jonathan fled from the battlefield but the Philistines came after them. Jonathan was killed by an arrow and Saul was so badly wounded he knew he could not escape. He drew his sword and killed himself.

When David heard the news he tore his clothes to shreds as a sign of sorrow. He and his men ate no food till the evening. Together they mourned for Saul and his son. Then David picked up his harp and sang a lament for Saul and his dear dead friend, Jonathan:

Daughters of Israel, sorrow for Saul
who gave you brooches of gold and clothed
you so well:
Now he is dead on the battlefield; let no dew
or rain fall!

For Jonathan's dead and Saul's with him
lying:
they were swifter than eagles, far stronger than
lions;
dear to me, lovely, not divided in dying.

High on the mountains our heroes all fell.
Why did your weapons fail you, O Israel?

Then the people of Israel made David king and he rebuilt Saul's kingdom, but he had no capital city until one day when he and his men went to attack a fortress which belonged to Israel's enemies, the Jebusites.

'You'll never capture us,' jeered the Jebusites. 'We've built our fort on solid rock. There are steep precipices on three sides of us, and the walls on the fourth side are too strong for you.'

They were right, but there was one way into the city, and David discovered it.

'They've dug a secret tunnel right under the walls to their water supply outside the fort,' he told his men. 'We can go up it.'

Some of the soldiers crawled along a channel that led up a steep shaft in the rock and along a tunnel right into the fortress. They opened the gates and let the rest of David's army in.

So David captured the fortress and built his capital city there. Its name was Jerusalem and there is a city on this spot to this day. From Jerusalem David ruled his kingdom and made it strong.

David didn't forget his friend Jonathan. One day he asked Saul's old servants if anyone in Jonathan's family was left alive. 'If so, I'd like to help them in some way for Jonathan's sake,' he said.

'There is someone,' replied one of the men. 'He's Jonathan's son, sir. He's lame.'

'Fetch him here to me,' David ordered, and the men went to look for him.

Some days later the servants announced: 'Here is Mephibosheth, Jonathan's son!' Mephibosheth limped slowly into David's room. He greeted David politely and knelt in front of the king. David could tell that he was frightened. He spoke gently to his best friend's only son. 'Don't be afraid, Mephibosheth. I haven't brought you here to harm you, but to see if I can help you. I'm going to give you back all the farms which your grandfather Saul owned. You shall have servants to look

after them for you.' Mephibosheth looked up at David in amazement.

'I'm too lame to fight for you, sir, and my grandfather kept trying to kill you. I thought you would treat me as your enemy. Why are you so kind to me?'

'Your father was my truest friend,' answered David.

From then on Mephibosheth had an honoured place in David's palace and ate all his meals at the king's own table.

David always looked for ways to please
God. The people of Israel had a box which
their ancestors had made long before when
they followed their leader Moses across the
desert. They put the commandments God gave
them inside the box and treasured it, for God
himself had said that his presence would
always be specially near it. David wanted to
honour God and so he decided to give the
precious box a new home in Jerusalem. He and
his men marched in a splendid procession to
fetch it. David felt so happy he began to dance.
He took off his royal robes and leapt and
danced with all his might while his people
watched. His wife Michal saw him. 'David's
making a fool of himself dancing like that in
front of everyone,' she thought and she
scolded him about it when he got home. But
David didn't care. He knew that he had
danced in praise of God, and that God was
pleased with him.

After the box was safely in Jerusalem David
held a great feast. Everyone in the city received
bread and cakes of dates and raisins to eat.

David is remembered as the best king Israel
ever had.

David finally defeated all his enemies and became rich and powerful. He built himself a palace in Jerusalem of trimmed stone and cedarwood and he lived there with his family. Although he was busy governing the kingdom and building the city, he still tried to remember that it was only through God's help that he had become king. He would pick up his harp and sing songs about the ways God had helped him, when his life had been in danger and he had been alone and unhappy. We can still read in our Bibles the words David wrote so many centuries ago. We call them the Psalms.

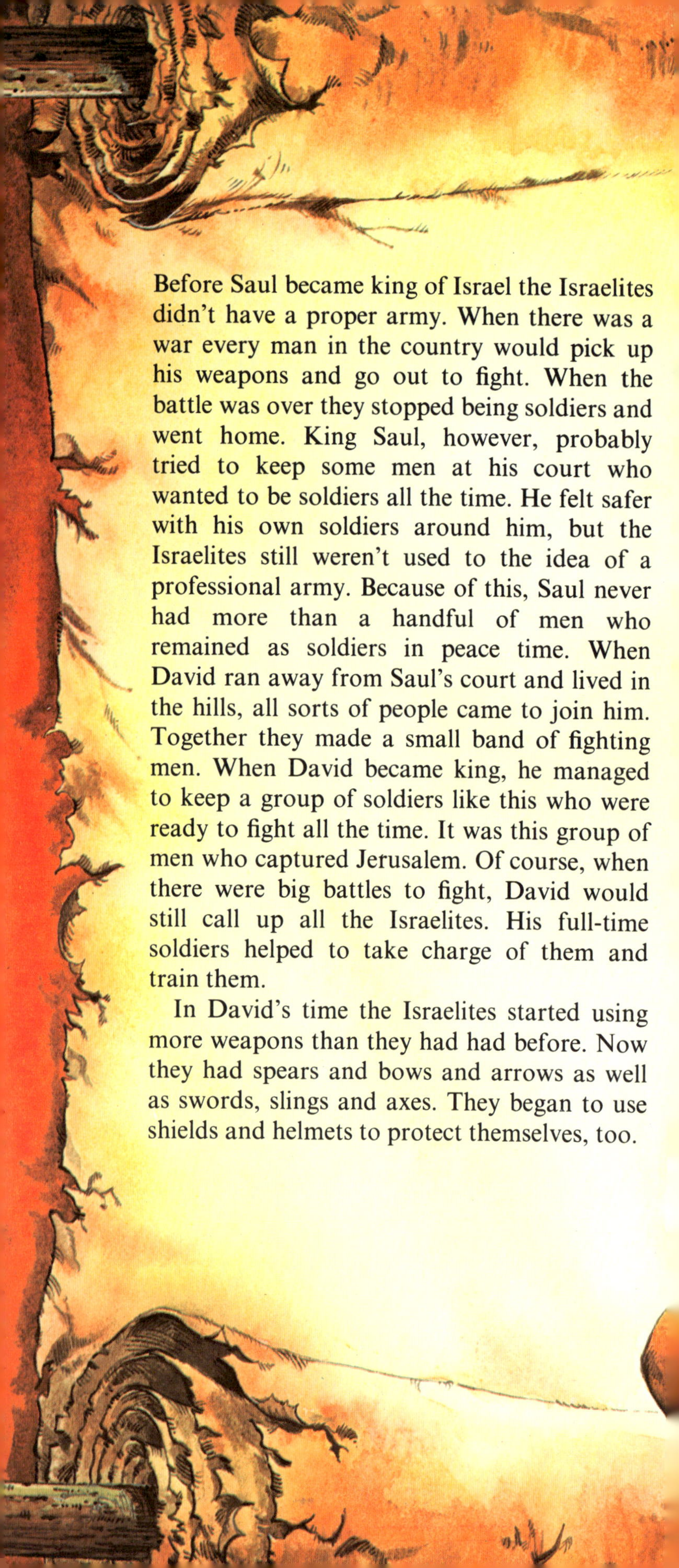

Before Saul became king of Israel the Israelites didn't have a proper army. When there was a war every man in the country would pick up his weapons and go out to fight. When the battle was over they stopped being soldiers and went home. King Saul, however, probably tried to keep some men at his court who wanted to be soldiers all the time. He felt safer with his own soldiers around him, but the Israelites still weren't used to the idea of a professional army. Because of this, Saul never had more than a handful of men who remained as soldiers in peace time. When David ran away from Saul's court and lived in the hills, all sorts of people came to join him. Together they made a small band of fighting men. When David became king, he managed to keep a group of soldiers like this who were ready to fight all the time. It was this group of men who captured Jerusalem. Of course, when there were big battles to fight, David would still call up all the Israelites. His full-time soldiers helped to take charge of them and train them.

In David's time the Israelites started using more weapons than they had had before. Now they had spears and bows and arrows as well as swords, slings and axes. They began to use shields and helmets to protect themselves, too.